NINA CAMPBELL

ELEMENTS OF

Design

NINA CAMPBELL

ELEMENTS OF

Design

elegant wisdom that works for every
room in your home

words by
ALEXANDRA PARSONS

CICO BOOKS
LONDON NEW YORK

747
CAM

This edition published in 2013
First published in 2007 by CICO Books
an imprint of Ryland Peters & Small Ltd.
20—21 Jockey's Fields
London WC1R 4BW
519 Broadway, 5th Floor
New York, NY 10012

10 9 8 7 6 5 4 3 2 1

A CIP catalog record for this book is available from the Library of Congress and the British Library.

ISBN: 978 1 78249 036 4

Printed in China

For digital editions, visit
www.cicobooks.com/apps.php

Photography by Paul Ryan
except for the following:

Tim Beddow p 6 top right, middle center; pp 47, 48, 49, 68, 103–107, 144–147, 148, 154–161
Christopher Drake pp 3, 6 (bottom left) 46, 69, 70–73, 96–101, 108–113, 128–129, 150–153
Douglas Friedman pp 91–95
Phillip Ennis pp 10, 162–163

Editor: Alison Wormleighton
Concept design: Christine Wood
Designer: David Fordham
Floor plans: Stephen Dew

contents

introduction

Styles in decorating come and go, but my philosophy has always been pretty consistent. My personal taste is for a house that is glamorous, comfortable, and easy to live in and reflects the lifestyle and personality of the owner. But I do not live in the past. Today's technologies give the designer an unbelievable amount of scope, and houses can be warmer, cooler, lighter, and brighter than they ever were. Today, virtually everything you think of you can do (except influence the dragons in the planning department).

The starting point for this book is a massive conversion I undertook on my own house. Apart from its location and the fact that I could carve out a garden for my dogs, the house I bought had absolutely nothing to recommend it. So I was able to gut it and start from scratch, to visualize the way I wanted to live within the space, and then set about making it work. Being my own client for well over a year was an interesting experience and it forced me back to the basics, to the elements of design that make a house work.

LEFT AND ABOVE:
Once the space makes sense and the bones of your scheme are in place, then is the time to delight in beautifully crafted details of design, from inlaid furniture to handmade trimmings and color-coordinated flowers.

7

RIGHT: *Even the most elegant furnishings can also be practical. In the summer the turquoise and gold cut velvet seats of these dining chairs in a house in Greece are given cool, washable linen slip covers in aqua linen with brown edging.*

LEFT AND BELOW LEFT: *.An outdoor seating area near a pool. It is no bad thing to bring a sense of order and calm to outdoor spaces as well as indoor ones. The furniture is a charming mix of modern outdoor furniture with the clients' retro "patio sets" which give a Hollywood feel.*

The place to start, of course, is with the space: the relationship between the different functions of the house and the sources of sunlight and fresh air. Then there is the question of storage—no house-builder ever creates enough storage. Once these basic bones are in place, along with provision for lighting and heating, then and only then is the time to think about creating the atmosphere you have had in mind all along. As a designer you have to juggle all these elements in your head at the same time, holding on to your vision and working your way toward it.

I hope that this book, which showcases work I have realized not only for myself but for clients all over the world, will give you an insight into the essential elements of design and inspire your projects to greater heights. On the other hand, if it only moves you to rationalize your closets, I shall still feel it has all been worthwhile.

ABOVE LEFT AND ABOVE RIGHT: *Good lighting is crucial in every room, and you need to plan it right at the beginning of any refurbishment in case new wiring is necessary. Both of these bedrooms have adjustable wall lights on swing arms for reading in bed, and the bedroom above right also has a bedside lamp to provide ambient lighting.*

RIGHT: *This wonderful mirrored art deco four-poster is in a large master bedroom suite in a New York apartment. The bed itself is dressed in a self-patterned cream voile, which allows the silk curtains at the window to be the decorative feature. This gives the room a contemporary edge.*

my open-plan space

I never meant to buy the house. It was a neglected, scruffy

building tucked away at the blind end of a street.

All I could see from the outside was a sad-looking hut, and

as I wrestled with the front door there was more gloom to

come—the dark ground floor had no redeeming features,

apart from an unworkable kitchen in the wrong place.

Then I made my way upstairs to the tiny top story and,

peering down through that window onto sunlit greenery, I

was beginning to see that the hut was, in fact, an urban

space with potential.

LEFT AND ABOVE: *It was the view from the bedroom that sold the house to me. A magnolia tree brushes up against the window—it's a wonderful view to wake up to.*

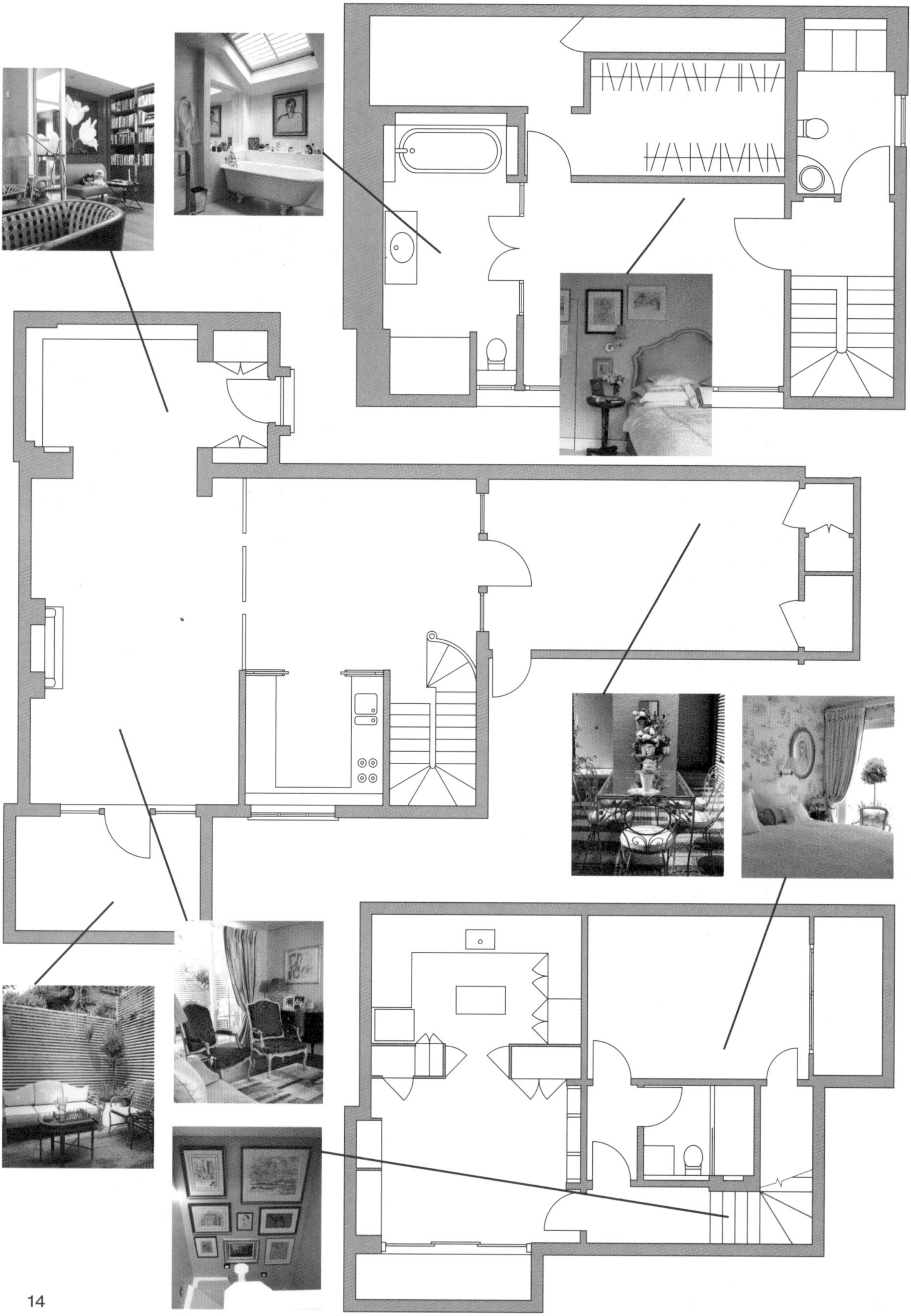

making the space work

The key to making the house work for me was to make it bigger. There was no way I could extend upward because of neighbors and planners. So I looked at extending downward. I realized that if I could dig out a basement and hive off the guest room and TV room, as well as what they call in hotels the "back of house" functions, such as laundry and storage for things like linens, platters, cleaning materials, and wine storage, I could claim the two existing floors for myself and my prodigious entertaining habit.

It was an ambitious plan, but once I knew that the house had to be completely gutted, it was a great opportunity to rewire and replumb, replace all the windows and the roof, get rid of the incipient damp, and rationalize the varying floor levels so the spaces could flow without impediment.

You enter into a blast of color. The paint shade, *Cassis*, is part of my paint range. We used it as the base from which John Sumpter, with whom I have worked all my design career, mixed a wonderful deep blackcurrant lacquer. It goes with the *Orleans* damask on my father's chairs (pictured on pages 18–20), which are positioned against the window at the far end of the living

ABOVE: *The dramatic entrance area is a foretaste of colors to come in the living area. I used panels of mirror glass to bounce the light around.*

ABOVE: *My house is big on storage. Here, useful cupboards are set beneath the bookshelves.*

RIGHT: *My dogs are one of the main reasons for buying a house with a garden. Here, Archie and Theo are comfortable on a banquette beneath a painting by Sophie Coryndon. The alabaster sculpture on the Plexiglas stand is* The Penguin *by Ally Brown.*

space, so the color is carried through. This gives it a more vibrant surface. I put thin columns of antiqued glass into the run of bookcases to bounce light from the glass roof and offer tantalizing glimpses of the garden. There are huge cupboards either side of the front door, one to house all the meters and electrics and one for coats and boots, so there is no excuse for clutter.

Being just off the living area, it is a nice place to sit. I have a drinks tray here, so I can serve guests a predinner cocktail without fuss. A pair of full-length antiqued mirror panels, which shuffle light from one space to another, mark the transition to the living area, where the predominant colors are aqua and amethyst. The walls are upholstered in an aqua linen painted in silver, which gives a wonderful gleam.

LEFT: *As a child, I used to sit in these chairs, curled up against my father, so they have enormous sentimental value for me. I upholstered them in my* **Orleans** *damask. The over-scaled pattern reminds me of their original owner—larger than life.*

the living areas

My vision for the ground floor was to create an open-plan, light-filled, shimmering living space with two courtyard gardens leading off it and an elegantly simple and basic kitchen that could be screened from view when required. And that is what I now have.

The fireplace is the focal point, as indeed it should be. I bought the brass art deco mantelpiece in New York. It was a bit too wide, so I devised the mirrored slips to make it fit. Then I discovered a problem with the size of the flue, so there was no way I could have a functioning fireplace. I opted instead for an Alice in Wonderland illusion, installing a basket of rock crystal logs, which when lit from above look just magical.

Surrounding the fireplace is an eclectic mixture of seating. I have a pair of small satinwood tub chairs to the right of the fireplace. The sofa is from Niermann Weeks. Dominating the view are two magnificent chairs from my father's house. The lighting is flattering and subtle—there's nothing as glamorous as the glow from a shirred silk chiffon lampshade. The lamps are sitting on a pair of black lacquer Biedermeier chests, which offer yet more storage.

ABOVE LEFT: *I like mixing styles and periods. Here my grandmother's Victorian coffee service sits alongside modern saucerless cups on a 1930s tray.*

ABOVE: *An artwork of gilded lotus leaves hangs above the fireplace with its rock crystal logs.*

PREVIOUS PAGES: *The curtains, made from one of my new fabrics,* Balzac, *link all the colors. They hang simply on Plexiglas poles so there is nothing to stop the eye.*

the dining room and kitchen

The house has low ceilings, and I have a floor of lovely wide smoked-oak boards. I could sense an acoustic disaster in the making, so the walls of my living space have one of my fabrics stretched and battened onto them not only because I like the look of fabric on walls but because it is practical. Padded fabric creates a dense, deadening effect so music and voices are enhanced and there is no reverberation. I have a simple but effective sound system: an iPod dock in the kitchen wired up to speakers in the ceiling, so there is no tower of power with trailing wires or CD storage problem.

The mirror-fronted piece of furniture in my dining room came from my apartment, where the base had been covering a long radiator, and as a result was too tall for this house. I asked William Yeoward to redesign the cupboard using the original top but with a new cupboard base, giving me much-needed extra storage space, and he has done an incredible job. It is more than a cupboard—it is a work of art, and the antiqued glass in the doors casts flattering reflections and makes the most of candlelight.

My dining table (with an extension) seats fourteen. It, too, came from my old apartment and it works for me as it is long and narrow and very good for conversation. I gained a bit of space here by recessing the radiators into the wall. I could have installed underfloor heating, but the dogs do not like it, so that was that.

RIGHT: *The dining table in action. The mirrored panels of my William Yeoward cupboard give the space—which is essentially a long thin slice of room—a new dimension.*

LEFT AND ABOVE: *The cut-glass centerpiece holds a cascade of flowers that tumble onto the table in the dining room. Pinks, blues, and purples recall the color theme of the open-plan area. The cranberry Venetian glasses have been favorite items at my shop for thirty years.*

My next project is to install a sliding sculpted glass panel that will hide the dining area so my guests will get a surprise when the screen is pulled back to reveal the beautifully laid table, and after dinner it can be shut to hide the abandoned meal. Too much open-plan leads to a lack of hazard and surprise which are key elements of good design and good entertaining.

Although my kitchen is small, I have as much space as I need because I can store all the bulky items in the utility room in the basement. Consequently, it is a highly efficient space and a joy to use. With the sliding doors open, the kitchen looks like an alcove off the dining area—shiny, lacquered, and elegant, with a windowsill lined with flower vases. I asked Kitchens Plus, the company who installed the kitchen, to make panels for the walls to match the cupboards, so the whole room is like a lacquered box with panels of mirror glass filling in between the tops of the cabinets and the ceiling. And with the sliding doors shut, you would not even know that the kitchen was there.

ABOVE: *My kitchen is compact but practical. Downstairs in the utility room I have all the space I need to store oversized platters, flower vases, fish kettles, and the like that so often have to clutter up a working space. I also have wine storage down there and an immense fridge.*

LEFT AND RIGHT: *The courtyard that gives onto the living area does not catch much sun, so this is essentially my evening terrace, where dinner guests can enjoy a drink outdoors. Moroccan lanterns hang from the wooden slatted fencing, and the candlelight shining through the pierced lanterns creates a romantic glow.*

BELOW LEFT: *The courtyard leading into the dining area gets flooded with sunlight and is a great place for a summer lunch or breakfast.*

the courtyards

The smaller courtyard garden that the living area opens onto has a retractable awning above it so I can close it off and turn the space into an exotic desert tent. I often do this for dinner guests, strewing the tiled floor with rugs and lighting candles in the pierced brass lanterns. I have given my little garden complete privacy with a high wooden slatted fence that lets in air and light.

The larger courtyard garden runs off the dining room. The horizontal lines of pebbles and limestone make the long, narrow space look wider, and the

LEFT: *The glass and metal table and chairs were a real find. They are original American 1950s garden furniture that I had resprayed. I had the cushions made in a magnolia print, in keeping with the theme of the house. The wooden slatted fencing is painted in a soft shade of gray-white from the Paint & Paper Library. I named the color* Rita Says *after my daughter Rita.*

ABOVE RIGHT: *Details of the table setting, pierced silver chargers from Morocco, and green glass bowls and plates—perfect for a green and white themed garden area.*

RIGHT: *One of the magnolia print cushions, a perfect color match for the newly sprayed chairs.*

BELOW RIGHT: *Little pots of greenery march down the center of the table.*

little building at the end hides trash cans and a storage area (more storage— can you ever have enough?) for cushions and gardening essentials. Both of the courtyards are responsible for delivering light and air to the two principal rooms in the basement, via pierced cast iron grilles and reinforced glass panels let into the floor.

I have rolldown metal shutters that seal off the interior from the gardens, making it a completely secret house. When it is all shut up, no one would ever know what was inside—very Alice in Wonderland!

ABOVE: *The small guest bathroom has a generous shower. Better to have a huge shower than to cram a mean bath into a tight space. Porthault towels add splashes of color.*

LEFT: *Looking down the new staircase from my bedroom. The watercolors and drawings are all linked through their meanings for me and always give me pleasure as I go down the stairs. At top left is a watercolor of my first drawing room, in which you can just make out the wall sconce that I now have in my dining room (see page 23). The watercolor at top right is by Paul Maze. At bottom right is a Ballets Russes fabric, and the small portrait sketches are of Diaghilev and Léon Bakst.*

LEFT AND ABOVE: *The black and gold extravaganza that is my guest powder room. The uneven oval brass sink sits on a Belgian black slate corner cabinet, for which the paint finish, devised by John Sumpter, is a mixture of silver and gold to pick up the gold leaves in the wallpaper. The almost invisible door gives access to further storage.*

upstairs and downstairs

In a corner of the house I added a new staircase. There are directional lights at floor level, so there's no need for awkward spotlights angled from the ceiling, and the lighting is safe and subtle. Stairs are a great place to hang prints or collections of pictures that mean something to you—after all, that's the point of hanging them.

The stairs lead down to the TV room, utility room, and guest bedroom, which has a small white shower room, and up to the master bedroom and bathroom, and a guest powder room. The powder room is a tiny, dark, misshapen room under the eaves, so I have used my *Magnolia Campbellii* wallpaper to make it darker, richer, and more glittery, while disguising the uneven contours. It always gets a reaction. I love it.

the guest bedroom

The guest bedroom gets its light and air from the courtyard off the dining room, and has sliding glass doors opening into the light well. It has an extremely comfortable bed and top-of-the-range linen—I think there is nothing more welcoming. It also has a huge closet that goes right back under the stairs, so there is plenty of room to stow suitcases as well as generous hanging space. The wallpaper on the walls and the fabric on the headboard and chairs is my take on a toile de Jouy, only this is a London toile. I call it *Promenade* as it reminds me of my childhood in Hyde Park. This is a small room, and the color scheme is consistent and restful. I reused a lavender wool rug from my apartment, which is repeated in the pale lavender paint, from my collection at the Paint & Paper Library, used for the walls of the small guest bathroom (see page 30) and also the walls of the light well.

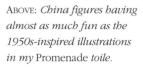

ABOVE: *China figures having almost as much fun as the 1950s-inspired illustrations in my* Promenade *toile.*

LEFT: *The light well floods the guest bedroom with light. The doors slide open so it is possible to step outside for a breath of fresh air, courtesy of the metal grilles set into the floor of the courtyard above. The grilles also mean that the sliding doors can be left open without security worries. The bay trees and lavender add a sense of depth and perspective, and I am still looking for two huge, old-fashioned, outdoor mirrors to serve the same purpose.*

ABOVE RIGHT: *Detail of the Louis XV chair upholstered in the* Promenade *toile. I picked specific scenes to center on the seat and the back.*

RIGHT: *The dressing table, which I bought in Paris, is of parchment-covered wood. It is an unusual and favorite piece of mine, and its curvaceous lines and creamy color fit perfectly into this bedroom.*

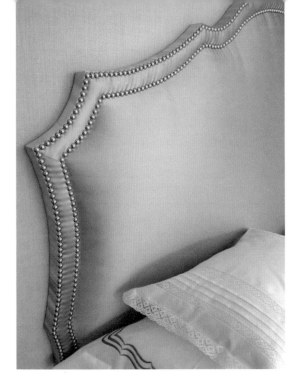

ABOVE LEFT: *Silver close nailing emphasizes the glamorous shape of the headboard upholstered in a pale gray satin.*

the master bedroom

When I first saw the house, I realized I wanted to sleep facing the magnolia tree, which meant I had to flip the bedroom and bathroom around and make the dormer window larger. It was worth the trouble.

The bedroom and bathroom are lit from skylights and windows, so the combined space is always flooded with light during the day. The walls are covered in a pale pink linen, and the scheme is accented with Dior gray. On the folding doors leading to the bathroom I have used antiqued mirror glass, which is softly flattering. I do not stint on bedlinen: it is one of life's simpler luxuries, and I think a bed should actually look as comfortable as it feels.

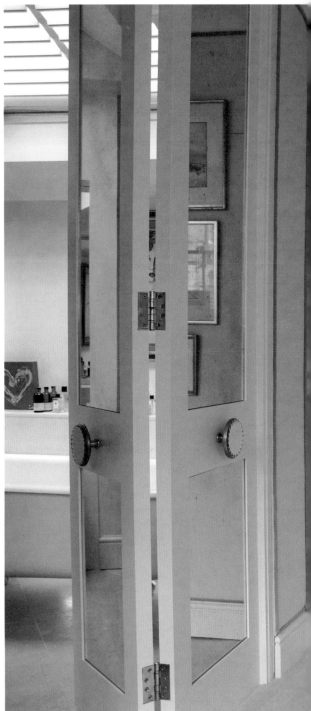

ABOVE: *A door leading to a walk-in closet, which runs the length of the house under the eaves, is decorated to blend into the background.*

ABOVE: *The bedroom is the place for personal photographs and mementos. I bought the painting of Mother Teresa and the monkeys because I loved it and it reminded me of my trip to India.*

LEFT: *This is a* Millais *chair from my furniture collection. It was actually designed as a fireside chair but it looks good in my bedroom. I upholstered it in* Kew Green, *a linen from my collection, which pulled together the color scheme.*

The pictures in the bedroom are all very personal to me. There are dancers and beach scenes and there is a watercolor by Cecil Beaton of my godmother, so I am surrounded here by good memories. The *Monkeys* triptych hanging above the chest of drawers is by a dear friend of mine, Sunita Kumar, an artist who worked closely with Mother Teresa. It has very good vibrations.

In the master bathroom (see overleaf), the walls are painted in a pale pink lacquer that exactly matches the linen-covered bedroom walls. A sink is inset into a mirrored buffet, which we extended backward to make it deep enough and to accommodate the plumbing. We silverleafed the wood and then painted a pink glaze over it, giving a translucent, mirrored effect. A piece of furniture can often be adapted to house a sink, and this one worked well, particularly as the drawers and cupboards offered so much storage space.

ABOVE: *Here you can see the reason I bought this house: the magnolia tree that brushes up to my bedroom window. The bookcase under the window conceals an air-conditioning unit.*

37

LEFT: *My bathroom is a delight of mirrors. The sink is housed in a 1930s buffet that we adapted, silverleafed, and then glazed.*

RIGHT: *The bathroom is lit from a skylight so the quality of light is always good. The Victorian bath, the only item salvaged from the original house, is set in an alcove beneath the skylight, affording a splendid view of a grand plane tree growing near the house. I love my daughter's portrait that hangs over the bath, and it will not be damaged by steam as the bathroom is well ventilated and never gets too steamy.*

ABOVE AND RIGHT: *One of the secrets of the success of this house is the utility room in my newly excavated basement. This is the linen closet where I store my table linens— tablecloths on hangers so that they get less creased, and napkins neatly sorted into sets.*

in conclusion

My mantra has always been "Get the space right first." There is no point in painting a wall a divine shade of purple if the wall should not be there in the first place. I spent a year living in my new house getting to know it better—and during that year my plans evolved. Sometimes I compromised and other times I saw potential that had eluded me at first. I learned to respect the compact spaces that forced me to come up with some serious lateral thinking and in return I have been rewarded with a slice of leafy urban delight, tucked away from view, that is a total surprise from the minute you walk in and continues to surprise and enchant as you journey through it.

RIGHT: *Shoes. Well, you have to put them somewhere, and if you have the space, better to see what you have than resort to a jumble at the bottom of a cupboard. I treated myself to fifty pairs of matching shoe trees in varying shades of pale linen. The shoes seem happy and it makes me take more care of them.*

entrances and exits

The hallway sets the tone of the house and deserves to

be considered as a space with a character of its own

rather than just a point of transition to somewhere else.

In the eighteenth century it was considered appropriate

to make hallways as restful and tranquil as possible to

soothe arriving travelers after their hellish journeys, hence

the traditional cool restraint of black and white floor tiles.

However, there's always a case to be made for a bold,

dramatic welcome.

LEFT: *This hallway is dramatic and soothing at the same time. Hovering on a Plexiglas shelf above the black and gold Regency cabinet is a massive spinach-green jade Buddha. Flanking the cabinet is a pair of Klismos chairs. All this is set against a gold paper-backed silk wall covering.*

RIGHT: *A paneled lobby off the entrance hallway is painted spinach green in deference to the jade Buddha. Beyond the mirrored double doors is a powder room.*

ABOVE: *A pierced concrete jalousie screen lets in light and air. It is veiled with sheer linen held top and bottom.*

ABOVE RIGHT: *Either side of the Buddha are a pair of silver and mirror-glass planters with white hydrangeas.*

a cool retreat from the heat

The hallway pictured overleaf and above is in a Greek house that had been built in the 1960s and was in need of a major update. The starting points here were the green jade Buddha, which I felt deserved a suitably regal setting, and the lovely black and gold Regency cabinet. The walls are covered in a gold-colored paper-backed silk, and the floor is the original black and white marble tile. Picking up on the Buddha, the woodwork is painted with dark green lacquer. We installed mirror panels all around the room to bring in light, and they also reflect the art deco light fixture. It is a soothing and cool environment, where you can immediately shake off the heat of the day. Of course, there is a huge coat closet (an essential in every hallway). A large powder room beyond the mirrored doors has a sink set into a mirrored cabinet that was made to fit (see pages 164–5).

Red is a great base color

halls with drama and impact

This is the hallway of a ground-floor apartment without a light source of its own. It was essential to create a powerful first impression and to make people feel instantly welcome as soon as the door opens.

If you have read any of my previous books, you'll know that red is one of my favorite colors, and that I think of it almost as a "neutral" because it works with virtually any kind of decorative treatment. It is a marvelous background for pictures, too.

I used a color scheme of red, cream, and gold to complement the magnificent living room carpet visible through the doorway. To give this narrow hallway drama and sparkle there is a wonderful Venetian mirror that belonged to the client and a gilt and marble console table. It all adds up to a definite wow factor. The stairs lead down into the hall from the front door on the floor above and I wanted to make it an inviting journey. There's a white carpet, which works in an apartment because by the time you get there you have gotten rid of the dust on your shoes.

LEFT: *The console table in the hallway makes a big dramatic statement but it is also surprisingly practical. Situated opposite the kitchen door, it becomes a landing stage for drinks. A cut-glass vase is the perfect choice for this hall, faceting the light and adding sparkle. The two gilt urns just had to be there. If you are going to do drama, you have to do it properly.*

RIGHT: *The Venetian mirror in all its glory. It looks so marvelous because it is faceted, bouncing the light and pleasingly fractured images all over the place.*

the hallway as art gallery

LEFT AND ABOVE: We ran out of Sempé cartoons, but rather than race out and acquire more, we found a striking Mickey Mouse in the owner's collection of prints. I think it is important to use what you have and in this case it was a fun mixture of styles and eras.

Hallways and staircases make great spaces for hanging pictures. If you are collectors, like these clients of mine, then hanging pictures close together shows off the collection in a way you can enjoy. These cartoons by the French artist Jean-Jacques Sempé are such fun that they make people want to dawdle on the stairs because there's always something different to be amused by. The walls have a self-stripe cream wallpaper to give the background a bit of movement, and the red runner on the stairs has a dark green decorative edging. You need to create a bit of discipline when close-hanging pictures.

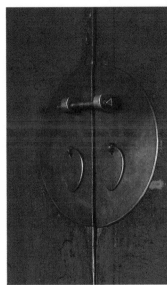

A landing with a practical surprise

ABOVE AND ABOVE RIGHT:
The antique Chinese cabinet
on the landing hides its practical secrets and adds to the general ambience.

RIGHT: *The secrets revealed. You can prepare a pitcher of Pimm's or a tray of coffee, or rinse a wine glass without running up and down the stairs, and it consequently makes the roof terrace a more beguiling place to be.*

furnishing landings

Going on up the staircase that has the Sempé cartoons lining the walls, the stairs deliver you onto this landing where the principal bedrooms are. The next floor up is the roof terrace, a delightful place to linger with a drink, but a considerable distance from the kitchen. The problem was neatly solved with the purchase of a lovely antique Chinese wardrobe. The distressed red/gold lacquer finish worked perfectly with the abundance of gilt frames and the cream wallpaper. But more interestingly, it is positioned with its back to the bathroom so it was possible to discreetly plumb in a small sink and wire up an outlet. The cupboard becomes a treasure chest of delicious treats.

CHAPTER THREE

LEFT: *Not so much a coffee table, more a work of art. The items on this glass surface are constantly edited, tidied, and realigned as if this were an installation in an art gallery. Notice how the strong graphics—the reds and yellows and silver accents—tell a story.*

living areas

Living rooms are for living in. The days of the stiff, gracious —and barely used—formal drawing room are limited, and today's living spaces are fluid and comfortable. Now that the barriers are down and rooms are spaces—spaces to entertain, relax, maybe work, or eat—it is important to zone your activities. Imagine how the room will work when it is being used for entertaining guests or by the family. Plan the space first and make architectural changes if necessary. Here I've created rooms that flow comfortably through from lobby and dining room to the living area, perfect for parties but also for relaxing at home.

Inviting a painting into your life

the starting point

While the installation on the modern glass and brass coffee table is certainly an artwork in itself, this room is dominated by a major Renaissance painting with a huge impact. We based the entire scheme around it—what else could you do? We took the fireplace out in order to hang the painting in pole position and, inverting tradition, built out the bookcases on either side. These hold not only books but also the television.

The Aubusson carpet was luckily flirting within the same color palette as the painting with its reds, creams, and golds. The walls are painted a non-color: a greeny-putty shade reminiscent of the stone pillars in the painting. The damask of the curtains—Orleans, from my collection—gives the scheme a decorative lift.

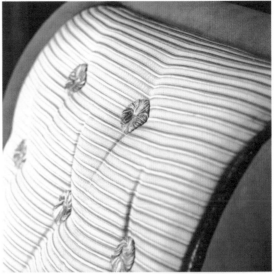

TOP AND ABOVE: *The chairs are my very comfortable Lamartine button-backs upholstered in red suede, ribbed silk, bead rim, and handmade fringe.*

LEFT: *With four windows, there is very little wall area here. When a room has a lot of window space, the curtains could overwhelm when closed. A good solution is to use lavish dress curtains, such as these in my* Orleans *damask lined in a dramatic color, and simple silk draw curtains.*

ABOVE: *The round display table has a glass top so it can be used to perch a drink on. The table lamp has a shade of pleated silk chiffon and gives the table arrangement some height.*

RIGHT: *The contrasting lining (in a man-made silk to prevent sun fading), draped over a contemporary Plexiglas tie-back, adds a splash of color without overwhelming the scheme. Pale pink roses in a simple silver vase complete the picture perfectly.*

making the space work

This is not an enormous room, but it works hard for its size. I set a two-seater sofa and a three-seater sofa at right angles to one another, and then placed a huge glass coffee table (pictured on pages 54–5 and 57) at the center of the room.

Once these main pieces were established, it was a question of slotting in necessary side chairs and tables without crowding the room. In the corner between the sofas I used a simple round table, giving it a glass top, a lovely lamp and a skirt made of lavender silk to match the dress of the Renaissance lady in the painting pictured on page 57. The narrow glass side tables at the other end of each sofa are extremely useful pieces, as deep as a sofa but narrow enough to fit into a small space.

The colors and textures in this room are designed to be restful and luxurious. Nothing jars, and nothing overwhelms. The room is a happy marriage of modern materials—glass tables plus Plexiglas curtain poles and tie-backs—and classic style. It works really well.

LEFT AND ABOVE: *Floor levels were rationalized so the living and dining areas would flow easily from one to another. The alcove with the stunning tapestry is the transition point, with the promise of seriously stylish refreshment.*

Keep a space flexible

working with pattern

This lovely tapestry reminds me of an Hermès scarf. Almost floor to ceiling in height, it arrived quite late in the process of planning this room, so we had to jiggle around with the baseboards and coves to accommodate it. However, the impact of a piece like this is worth any amount of last-minute adjustment.

After all that effort it might seem a bit perverse to put a table in front of it, but the table we chose was a slender glass and brass structure as elegant as any sculpture. The color of the metal practically blends into the tapestry, and the streamlined shape insures that the pattern of the heraldic design is uninterrupted. It serves as a drinks table in an area that now links the living space to the dining area, so it is a welcome sight for guests. It is also very beautifully arranged with exquisite glassware and an eye for symmetry.

63

Get the basics right first

a dining space with attitude

Originally this dining room was a dark space and the floor was two steps higher than the living area. So before anything else was done, the floor levels were sorted out and light introduced thanks to a vaulted glass ceiling, from which hangs a wonderful Baccarat glass chandelier. A small door into the garden was widened, and there are now huge French doors that open out flat and glass steps leading down into the courtyard garden. These are practical because they let the light through into the room below.

Then we built generous floor-to-ceiling cupboards in each corner and there was still space for a lovely mahogany table that seats ten to twelve in comfort. The "cupboard" to the right of the windows is, in fact, a door that leads down three steps to the kitchen. It is a dining area that is as practical as it is elegant.

ABOVE: *Chic, simple continental place settings reveal the owners' impeccable taste.*

LEFT: *The clients have not yet found the chairs they want, so until that day comes, they are using old-fashioned party chairs—the kind a caterer would have used—fitted with smart cushions.*

RIGHT: *These curtains face a sunny courtyard and so are lined with an acetate fabric that will not rot in the sun.*

the finishing touches

When you have got the space right, then it is time to give the room its character. We battened a dramatic fabric, trimmed with a three-colored cord, to the walls to soften the acoustics—an important consideration in a wooden-floored room full of lively chatter and clinking glasses.

The cupboards in each corner hold all the china, glassware, and linen safely and neatly. I know I keep saying this, but well thought-out storage is a vital ingredient for an easy life.

LEFT: *The classic English look updated: The palette is modern, there are bold splashes of color, and there's not a hint of chintz.*

RIGHT: *Red is the dominant color in this room. It's fun to bring in touches of color in unexpected places, like this enamel-bordered photo frame.*

Updating the traditional drawing room

modern colors in a traditional setting

The classic English country house look is universally admired and copied, not just because it is grand but because it is also comfortable and welcoming and will never go out of fashion. In the wrong hands, however, the look can be overwhelmed with fuss and frills. You can avoid this by sticking to a palette of three major colors, such as the red, cream, and blues in this room. Making a big splash with one strong color strikes a contemporary note, and that function is fulfilled here with the big red sofas.

Keep pillows to a practical number—there's no point in making work for yourself fluffing them up all the time. Look for clean-lined furniture and keep surfaces free from too much clutter.

This is the country house look adapted for a London apartment, admittedly a grand London apartment with high ceilings and an impressive wall of windows that could take the full swag, cascade, and fringe. It is always fun to go the full distance with a curtain treatment like this. The trick is not to lose your nerve.

LEFT: *On the side table to the right of the fireplace are a beautiful but practical match-striker and an amusing antique crystal and silver jug. I cannot imagine what it was meant to pour—maybe a splash of spring water into a tumbler of single malt.*

BELOW LEFT: *A detail of the fringing which picks up all the colors of the room: cream, aqua, and red.*

RIGHT: *Pillows add color and texture and so do flowers. I am never haphazard about the flowers I choose for a room.*

tailored furniture

Sharp, tailored lines and defined color are what gives a traditional sofa like this its modern edge. Instead of being squashy, today's sofas have firm arms and backs. The pillows reflect the main color themes in the room, and their patterns are relatively restrained. Detailing on sofas, chairs, and pillows is understated.

Nevertheless, trimmings are enjoying a tremendous revival at the moment, which is very cheering as much of it is handmade to order and it would be terrible if the skills of these craftspeople were to die out. To finish off the sofas, we chose a graduated-bobble wool fringing, which incorporates the colors of the room.

The sofas are the classic "Howard" or "Bridgewater" design, which has been widely used and adapted over the years and which I believe is the most comfortable of all sofas. In this room we used one three-seater and one two-seater because we needed to have access to the French doors leading out to the terrace. A fender stool provides extra places to perch.

LEFT: *A braid finish detail on the arm of the French side chair.*

BELOW LEFT: *A bergère is a really useful chair as it can be moved about and is a vehicle for a more elaborate fabric than you might otherwise use.*

BOTTOM LEFT: *A gilded wooden stool covered in silk picks up the aqua tones in the carpet.*

adding the decorative touches

Prettiness is back in vogue again, I am pleased to say. The first task here was to get the major features in place: the cream walls, the smart tailored sofas, and the mantelpiece, which was not original to the apartment— I deliberately chose one with simple, strong lines.

Then it was time to add the decorative touches, to soften and individualize the room. This is someone's personal space, after all, not a hotel room. I went hunting for pretty things: charming Louis XV bergère chairs, footstools, and console tables. It is great fun to find old French chairs and upholster them in unusual or vintage fabrics, or to put an outrageously expensive fabric on just a chair seat for a touch of luxury. In this case, however, I went for silk brocades and damask with pretty stripes and touches of gold for sparkle.

Finishes are critical. Baseboards should be pristine—just because they are at floor level does not mean they will not be noticed. I sometimes paint my baseboards in a darker shade, such as a brownish-black, which can create a dramatic look. Door frames should be in the right style and fit for purpose, as should door handles, light switches, and electric outlets.

The finish on soft furnishings is another detail that it is important to get right. Cushions should be properly piped and trimmed, and upholstery finished with braid or gimp or even nails.

LEFT: *The fender is upholstered in a gaufrage leather.*

BELOW AND RIGHT: *Now that we have been through minimalism and come out the other side, it is great to find people who can still make the ornate fringes and tassels that give these silk damask curtains the necessary flair and drama to make them work.*

LEFT: *This low, squashy sofa is an example of brilliantly executed upholstery. What particularly matters to me is that the pattern joins perfectly. It is covered in one of my fabrics,* Curraghmore, *a bold velvet in purple, pink, cream, and green. The pillows are in a solid-color velvet with a contrast trim. The sofa is placed at one end of a relaxed TV room in a home in Greece that you can see more of on the following pages. A pale green silk wallpaper creates the background for a picture from my client's own collection and a pair of wall sconces. Flanking the sofa is a pair of gilded tub chairs, which belonged to the client and we had re-covered. I think it is important to use a client's existing possessions whenever possible.*

LEFT: *For the TV room (also shown on pages 74–5), I chose a green silk wallpaper, and one of my fabrics,* Pemberley, *for the windows. It is a silk that looks hand-painted and feels fresh and vibrant, and it incorporates all the colors from the striped sofa. The desk chair is in a bright magenta velvet.*

A cool take on tradition

a classic look for a '60s house

This was an exciting project. The house, which is in Greece, had been built in the 1960s and had not really been touched since then. My clients had some amazing works of art and a collection of vintage 1960s furniture that was too good to ignore. We sent the furniture back for restoration to the company that had originally made it and set about creating a brand-new feel for the rather dated house—classic and cool.

There is an enormous living area in the center of the house, with rooms leading off it, and I wanted to create a variety of areas that flowed well from one to another and that would, in the end, have a common identity. The color scheme was to be creams, golds, and greens with touches of pinks and purples. You can see the dramatic hallway of this house on pages 42–5 and the dining room on pages 114–19.

ABOVE: *Looking though to the living area. The painting in this amazingly ornate gilt frame is of an oriental subject painted onto glass and it shimmers in the sunlight.*

RIGHT AND PREVIOUS PAGES:
One end of the living room leads through to the dining room. The stools in this seating area are covered in the same fabric as used for the curtains —the pattern repeat fits them perfectly. The beaten-brass coffee table has a silverleaf top under glass.

a room for all seasons

One side of the spacious living area overlooks an enormous terrace, and there are seating areas at both ends of the room. At one end is a marble fireplace. Although Greece is very hot in the summer, it can get surprisingly cold in the winter, so we wanted to make this an inviting place to gather around a fire.

Because the room is immediately off the hallway with the gold silk wall covering and the black and gold Regency cabinet (see pages 42–4), we repeated the gold in the fabric used for the curtains and two stools, and in the gold chenille used for two of the sofas. We had the rug specially made in Tibet with a cream background, and a border and central motif in greens and golds.

Against the terrace wall were some alcoves, but because they stopped at the top shelf, they looked rather cramped. The solution was to put mirror glass in each alcove behind the shelves and a curved panel of mirror glass above, and then frame the new, generous shape with a custom-made architrave. It was a bit of architectural cheating that instantly made the room fool lighter and brighter and better proportioned.

ABOVE: *At the fireplace end of the living area, the facing sofas are upholstered in my pale gold chenille and the armchairs in cream. The punch comes from the four modern bergère chairs covered in a fresh green silk velvet.*

RIGHT: *A perfect choice of blooms for a room full of light and reflections—I love the stark simplicity of the bunch of white anthurium in a Lalique vase.*

ABOVE: *The display of rock crystal in the mirrored alcoves is lit by LED lights inset into the shelves. The front of each shelf has a mirrored inlay.*

ABOVE RIGHT: *The silvered tables make another wonderful surface for the display of crystal and amethyst shells.*

sparkling light

We filled the alcoves in the living room with a collection of rock crystal from Peter Adler. Crystals do not respond well to a harsh single source of light, so I carved a track out of each shelf and inserted a run of LED lights. These hidden lights cast a sparkling light upward and downward, lighting the entire display without producing any heat, and, of course, are reflected in the mirror behind the shelves.

The 1930s-inspired end tables at the fireplace end of the room were specially made from thick glass with scrolling beaten-brass bases. The combination of crystal, glass, mirror, gold, and silver means that everything about this room is rich, mellow, and glowing.

inside outside living

The joy of a consistent climate is that you can set up an outdoor sitting area and leave it be. The terrace outside the living area of the house in Greece is one such space, with a retractable awning that provides welcome shade when the sun is at its height. Although outdoor fabrics come in amazing prints and colors, I chose a palette of beige and cream. The fabrics are from a wonderful range that offers solid colors, stripes, and polkadots, and even includes a fun turtle design. The fabric will not fade in the sun and is resistant to light showers so it can stay out all summer long. The metal furniture is wild and witty. It is a collection of vintage garden furniture, which has been restored and repainted. For the more solid seating I chose upright white powder-coated aluminum sofas by McKinnon and Harris.

Generous in size, the terrace is divided into various conversation areas, exactly as if it were a large living room, with well-placed side tables and light sources. It makes for a very congenial living space, with small groups gathering in one place, larger groups in another. (The dining terrace is pictured on pages 122–5.)

ABOVE LEFT AND ABOVE: *1950s metal garden furniture gets a new lease on life. The fabric range allows for plenty of contrast and interest, and the polkadots are great fun.*

LEFT: *Fabric with a turtle design is used on the pillows, providing a cheerful addition to the metal sofa. Big fat candles in huge glass lanterns will burn steadily.*

RIGHT: *A view of the terrace and the garden beyond, which is reached through an arch in a neatly clipped hedge. This terrace is an ideal place to read, catch the sun, chat, and gather before meals. The planting near the terrace keeps to the color scheme.*

rooftop living space

This is the roof terrace of a house in central London, where outside space is a precious commodity. The colors used here are a gentle yellow ocher and a drab moss green, tones that do not shout or clash or attempt to outshine nature.

Any roof terrace has to be ultrapractical. Here, the painted wooden deck drains onto a sealed flat roof; the wooden furniture is of hardwood so it can stay out all year round; there is a large storage cupboard nearby for the cushions; and the railings are high enough to satisfy stringent health and safety requirements. It is a long way down to the kitchen, but you can see on pages 52–3 the solution we came up with—a staging post hidden in a Chinese cupboard on the top-floor landing.

LEFT AND ABOVE: *A roof terrace is a welcome eyrie among the treetops of this cityscape. This London one is practical as well as pretty.*

entertaining areas

On the following pages are photographs of two

commissions I recently undertook to breathe new life into

the private entertaining areas of two well-loved and iconic

institutions either side of the Atlantic: Grand Central Station

in New York and the Royal Albert Hall in London. They are

included here because you learn some important lessons

when dealing with a space that is a given (you cannot start

tinkering with the dimensions of a landmark) and for which

people have so many expectations.

LEFT: *The panels of the long bar at Grand Central Station*
are reminiscent of the leaded glass in the window, and I
matched the wood of the bar to the window frame.

ABOVE: *Intimate pools of light in this huge space are achieved with stylish uplights and wall-hung downlights with silk shades.*

RIGHT: *The seating area contains comfortable sofas and armchairs in color-related fabrics. This space can be used for private dining, but its main function is to celebrate this iconic building and evoke the glory days of first-class train travel.*

ABOVE: *The long bar of the Campbell Room at New York's Grand Central Station is dramatically set around the huge window. I used my glamorous Liszt bar stools, upholstered in a fake lizard skin, to make the bar a great place to linger luxuriously between trains.*

the Campbell Apartment

The bar known as the Campbell Apartment at New York City's Grand Central Station was used as an office and salon in the 1920s, '30s, and '40s by the tycoon John W Campbell (no relation). It was considered at the time to be one of the most remarkable offices in New York and it remains one of the city's unique and secret spaces. It is open to the public, with the unobtrusive entrance tucked behind Cipriani's.

The architectural details of this 3,500 square-foot (325 square-meter) space include an immense leaded glass window, a magnificent coffered ceiling, a minstrels' gallery, and a massive stone fireplace. I wanted to create areas of intimacy and make the long bar a glamorous, luxurious destination for travelers, in a Jack Vettriano meets Anna Karenina style.

FAR LEFT: *Detail of the grand coffered ceiling and the stone walls of the Campbell Apartment. This grandiose space is a New York landmark.*

LEFT AND RIGHT: *The new Campbell Apartment tartan, which is not authentic but is a decorative success. In the tortoiseshell-framed mirror you can catch a glimpse of the carpet, bordered in blue, which picks up the colors of the room.*

the starting point

The golds, reds, and blues in the decorated ceiling, the mellow stone of the walls, and the existing dark woodwork were the starting points for me. I decided the space needed a plaid so that it could live up to its Scottish associations. The authentic Campbell tartan is blue, green, and black, which would not have worked in this massive space, as it needed some vibrancy and warmth, so I decided to create a new one. The plaid I came up with is based on the grid of the authentic tartan, but more simplified and graphic, and I chose a true red—a great color to work with.

The reds, pinks, and yellows used in the Campbell Apartment look vibrant and work well together if handled with care. I wanted to create a luxurious feeling for the space, and I knew that color would help me achieve that. Imagine how drab the space would have been with polite neutrals or that old club standby, dark green leather.

LEFT: *The Jacob van Ruisdael landscape and the portrait of Henrietta Maria are displayed against a background of smart charcoal gray linen. The color palette is a restrained gray, cream, and azure blue.*

RIGHT: *A constant reminder of the Royal Albert Hall's namesake: a view though the window of the newly restored Albert Memorial.*

the Clive Room

London's Royal Albert Hall was opened in 1871 by a grieving Queen Victoria in recognition of the contribution her beloved husband Albert had made to the cultural life of Great Britain. The Clive Room, the room I was asked to refurbish and redecorate, had previously been an office. It has two grand windows overlooking the Albert Memorial, so there was a constant reminder of the cultural heritage I was dealing with.

The function of this newly refurbished space was to display some of the wonderful collection of paintings acquired by the Royal Albert Hall, many of which had been languishing in storage. My job was to create a background for these in a room that could be used as a private dining room or as a boardroom. The Jacob van Ruisdael landscape seen on the left was one of the paintings chosen. When it was cleaned and restored, a beautiful blue sky was revealed. It was a blue I was considering using anyway – the painting clinched it.

The classic new dining room

LEFT AND ABOVE: *The blues in the color palette range from azure blue to a glossy dark blue, picked up here in the flowers and decorative objects.*

RIGHT: *The table, specially commissioned, is, in fact, two tables. Each can seat eight people in comfort; when they are pushed together, there is room for twelve or more.*

definition and detail

The classic proportions of the room were easy to deal with, and thanks to built-in air conditioning there were no massive Victorian radiators to wrestle with. Because I was asked to create a slightly more modern look than elsewhere in the Albert Hall, I was able to use a charcoal gray linen on the walls. It is the perfect background for these beautiful old masters in their gilded frames, and was the basis of the restrained palette of charcoal gray, cream, and blue that I chose. The entrance lobby to the room is painted in a strong blue gloss, with cream-painted double doors leading you into this calm and elegant space. The cream and taupe carpet, from my collection and called *Rosalind*, has just enough movement and interest.

The dining chairs are upholstered in a smart, blue stamped velvet, and the dress curtains, which are never drawn, are edged with an eye-catching blue braid. A gilt fillet that has been used to finish off the edges of the fabric on the walls picks up the gilt of the frames. The room is a beautiful display box— a perfect frame for its national treasures.

TOP AND ABOVE: *The Vulliamy clock was loaned by the benefactor of this room, Colin Clive, a direct descendant of Clive of India. It has pride of place, along with its certificate of provenance, between the two windows.*

ABOVE LEFT AND RIGHT: *The color palette of gray, cream, and blue is evident in both photographs. The wall sconces delicately echo the gilt of the picture frames.*

The classic dining room revisited

formal entertaining today

The red dining room is part of our heritage. There is nothing quite like it for formal grandeur, summoning up images of the animated conversation above the cut-glass crystal, the sense of luxury and ease that makes every guest feel special. It is, without doubt, one of the pillars of what is referred to as "English style."

But even a national treasure needs a facelift from time to time, and here I have updated the traditional theme by giving the bookcases in this dining room a boxy contemporary outline. There is lots of storage under the shelves, too, and I have incorporated modern lighting so that the room could be used as a library or study by day. With so many functions, there needs to be a sense of discipline underpinning the decorative choices.

The drama is provided by the large painting hanging above the sideboard and by the strong lines of the bookcases flanking it. We have integrated these with the architecture of the room by building up the cove. The glamour comes from the table when it is set for dinner with crystal and candlelight. Other elements are simply stated. The curtains and chair seats are in a buff and red stripe, and the carpet in a neutral. These work well together, and the curtain styling is restrained and understated (see page 105). It is a room with "welcome" written all over it.

LEFT: *The starting point for the decoration of this room was the striking painting, which can be seen from the room beyond through the double doors. I like the over-scaling of the painting framed by the bookcases.*

lighting is the key

This is a dining room in a typical 1960s building with a hodgepodge of beams on the ceiling. It was therefore not possible to put lights into the concrete ceiling without a lot of doctoring. My solution was to build a false ceiling around the edge of the room to house downlights and a smoke alarm. It is unobtrusive and creates a raised center in the room which helps give a feeling of height.

All rooms need a variety of lighting: ambient, or background, lighting; task lighting for close-up work; and accent lighting to highlight special features. During the day this dining room receives a fair amount of natural light through the large window. In the evening, there is the soft overall glow from the downlights. The painting has a picture light of its own, and the shelves are lit with directional lamps on flexible stems.

ABOVE: *The classic table setting is enhanced by small objects and curios.*

RIGHT: *The walls and shelving are all painted the same shade of red —a lot of contrast would have made the room look too busy. Simple dress curtains, which are rarely closed, frame a floor-to-ceiling window.*

a contemporary use of pattern

This is the dining room in the London house of a young couple who wanted a classic dining room in a modern idiom that would segue with ease from their incredibly modern kitchen. We chose a palette of sleek steel. The wallpaper (*Magnolia Campbellii* from my collection) is a shimmering silver mica with a restrained, delicate design of stylized flowers. The curtain and the shade are in matching steel-gray taffeta lined in red and edged with a steel-gray glass bead.

It is an elegant, pretty room, but it is essentially simple. The porcelain and table linen are monochrome and the red flower heads in the single-stem vases echo the trim of the curtains. The circular mirror adds to the sparkle created by all the shiny surfaces.

LEFT: *A red velvet tablecloth,*
gold chargers, red glass plates,
and red linen napkins make
a dramatic background.
The glass cake stand holds
antique mercury balls.

Concoct a contemporary table

creating a sense of occasion

I adore devising different table arrangements, and I collect glass and china to mix and match, but you do not, in fact, necessarily need a vast store of plates to have fun. Tablecloths and mats, napkins, flowers, and accessories from around the house all have their part to play in creating an atmosphere. Setting a table is now a million miles away from simply getting out the wedding china and setting it according to formal rules.

Start by matching your approach to the occasion. A summer lunch demands light, pretty colors, and flowers, while guests at a winter dinner party will respond warmly to rich reds, oranges, and other hot colors. The color scheme in your room can be a starting point, but dressing a table is also an opportunity to give the room a slightly different look for the day—by adding vibrant colors, for example, to a calm, neutral room, or a touch of formality to a casual dining space.

Do not be constrained by what's available under the label "tablecloth." You can use almost any fabric—velvet, silk, antique linen, upholstery fabric, dress material, or even sheets or bedcovers. You can also have a tablecloth custom-made for the table, as we have here. Fabric remnants can be a source of something special, too.

Color and texture

ABOVE LEFT: *I wanted to make this cloth look like a flea-market find. Having found this beautiful gold-on-velvet border at Pierre Frey, I added it to a plain velvet cloth along with a gold metallic cord and a gold bobble fringe.*

ABOVE: *A traditional favorite for the table, the versatile rose can stand alone as a single bloom or nestle in a low clump in a crystal or silver bowl. Roses are lovely flowers to look down upon, even when overblown.*

flowers with finesse

With a red velvet tablecloth as a starting point, there is already a very strong element of color and texture and a classic feel to this table. To give it a contemporary edge, I chose red linen napkins instead of the more traditional white and restricted the table flowers to roses. I made a few red roses go a long way by placing one or two perfect flower heads in eight identical small vases. The table looks very festive in a restrained way because the color palette is restricted. Flowers for tables need care and forethought; you do not want to overwhelm the senses with a buzz of too many colors or overpowering scents.

RIGHT: *The contrasting textures of linen, velvet, silver, glass, and china provide richness and depth. Monogrammed table linen does not have to be white—you can have some fun by dyeing vintage linens in different colors, which can often add the clash that is needed to give life to a scheme.*

LEFT: *A silver vase, silver and crystal decanters, and modern pressed-glass tumblers are part of a table setting designed to catch the light that streams in from the French doors.*

RIGHT: *The rich red room takes on a completely different perspective in the daytime. It is amazing what a difference a white lace tablecloth can make.*

BELOW RIGHT: *A detail showing where the beautifully laundered white lace meets the embroidered skirt of the red velvet undercloth.*

same background, different look

Same red velvet tablecloth, same room, but a completely different tablescape. I have added an antique lace tablecloth over the velvet one, along with decorative glassware, white china, and a generous vase of parrot tulips, roses, and eucalyptus leaves. This would make a great setting for a lunch party. The oranges and reds in the flowers remind us this is a predominately red room, and the very strength of the surroundings dictates a certain low-key approach to color at the table.

Although I love tablecloths and the variety they afford, I also own an enormous range of tablemats, from delicate Brussels lace to brightly colored organzas that would not disgrace an Indian wedding. And sometimes I like to leave a beautiful table quite bare and enjoy the wood. It is all a question of mood—choosing the backdrop for your tablescape is very much like preparing a stage set.

Not every centerpiece has to be floral. You could use any distinctive grouping—artichokes, Easter eggs, antique mercury balls (as seen on pages 108–9)—just pile them up generously on a cake stand or in an appropriate bowl and make that the starting point for an inspirational table.

cool and understated

The starting point for this scheme in the dining room of the Greek house shown elsewhere in this book (see pages 42–5 and 74–87) was the wonderful figurative painting that now hangs along the long wall of the room. The painting of ships at the far end is strongly graphic but does not impose any new color accents. Throughout all the rooms we used a soft palette of greens, golds, and lavender, with mirror glass to reflect light and improve the proportions of the 1960s-built house. The classic mahogany dining table, which extends to seat up to fourteen people, was original to the house, as were the chairs. We upholstered the seats with a turquoise and gold cut velvet, built cupboards in the corners for china and glass, and disguised the door to the kitchen within the paneled walls.

The beveled mirror panels are carefully positioned to give all the diners tantalizing glimpses of beautiful things and to bounce light around the room. The chandelier and the turquoise *torchères* were rewired and fitted with French candle bulbs, which give out a soft glow.

ABOVE: *Early Chinese necklaces from Peter Adler are displayed against a paneled wall with gilt insets.*

RIGHT: *This turquoise torchère on a Plexiglas stand is reflected in a mirrored panel.*

PREVIOUS PAGES: *The table is set with white linen and china with a low centerpiece of white flowers. I keep using the words glow and sparkle when describing this house, but that is what it really does.*

Conjuring up atmosphere

ABOVE LEFT: *I would encourage my clients to do as I do, and collect sets of glasses not because they need them, but because they are beautiful and may be an inspiration when setting a mood at the table. These chunky cut-crystal glasses are a case in point, providing a light show in their own right.*

LEFT: *Classic shell-pattern silverware always looks good. The plates have a delicate rim of gold and blue, providing a hint of color.*

RIGHT: *Plain white linen tablemats define each place setting. They are beautifully hand-embroidered with an edging of drawn-thread work. The silver bowl that holds the centerpiece flowers adds to the general classic look. Imagine this table at night with the candlelight flickering. Magic.*

LEFT AND ABOVE: *We chose a refreshing green and white color theme for the kitchen. The alcoves in the wall cabinets were painted green, the cabinet door knobs are green glass, and the glass backsplash was professionally painted with green horizontal stripes. Green and white fabrics were used for the roman shade and the seating. The built-in banquette sits on top of much-needed storage drawers, and the end tables flanking it are built-in wine refrigerators.*

kitchens for today

The change in how we use our kitchens has been dramatic. Today we eat in them—practically live in them—and it is probably the single area of the house on which we spend the most money.

I would always recommend consulting a professional kitchen design company for the units and layout. However, it is your family and your lifestyle, so stick to your guns and never let anyone talk you into the latest fashion or novelty appliance for the sake of it.

This kitchen was opened out to create a dining space for breakfasts and informal meals. It leads onto the garden, and there is a skylight above the eating area, so the room is sunny and bright.

LEFT: *This terrace leads out from a formal dining room. A wall of greenery separates this convivial area from the rest of the garden, and while it is used mainly during the day, candles and electric lanterns make it an enticing space for informal dinners.*

A versatile dining terrace

LEFT AND ABOVE: *The brightly printed tablecloth suggested the floral decorations: hot pink and orange gerberas in a collection of bud vases.*

RIGHT: *A colorful lunch table set in a calm, cool, neutral space, focusing the attention on the meal itself.*

a dining terrace in the sun

Leading off the dining room of the house in Greece (see pages 114–19) is this sunny dining terrace. Shade is provided by a white retractable awning. The white powder-coated aluminum tables and chairs can be left out all year. The brightly printed fine cotton tablecloth is so cheerful that it set the theme for the lunchtime table setting, for which I used green glass plates and pink striped glasses from the Nina Campbell collection. The napkins are a rainbow collection of fine cotton organdy—all part of the fun. The joy of this space is that it can be given any look, depending upon the mood.

quiet areas

Everyone needs a retreat, somewhere to keep paperwork

and deal with it in peace and quiet. For a study area that

works, you need storage—sensible shelving and

cupboards that will take unsightly box files—along with a

desk that is fit for purpose and a comfortable chair.

LEFT AND ABOVE: *A corner of a spare room that also serves as a study. The sofa bed is framed by a good-looking set of built-in shelving that can accommodate files and paperwork as well as reference books. The red and cream color scheme creates a restful background.*

a study in a box room

This 8 foot (2.5 meter) square room is just big enough for a desk, a chair, and some shelving, but we made it work. Good working light is a priority, and every desk should have a flexible desk lamp such as this one. You should also have good ambient light in the room, as you need more than task lighting when working, otherwise your eyes will tire. You can never have enough storage, and in this built-in bookcase there is just enough room between desk and bookcase to pull out the filing drawers.

LEFT: *The fabric lining the walls is from my* Manchu *range, an amusing take on the* Willow *pattern. The edges are finished with cord that relates to the color inside the shelves. Small rooms need to be quite strictly coordinated or they will look even smaller than they are.*

RIGHT: *A built-in bookcase houses filing drawers below— note the contrasting dark paint lining the shelves. The chair already belonged to my client, and I love its fabulous gaufrage mohair fabric.*

BELOW: *The beautiful little inlaid desk, which has a lovely scroll front, goes perfectly with the chair. The cup and saucer are from my signature* Hearts *range.*

room to work

This paneled study houses a wonderful collection of icons, and the tone for the decoration was set by the exquisite icon over the desk. Space was not a problem, nor was there a storage problem, as there were already built-in floor-to-ceiling bookcases within the paneling. However, the room looked tired, and the real satisfaction here came from bringing back to life the paneling, desk, and side chairs. Wood is such a joy to restore because it emerges rich and glowing, like Cinderella.

The inlaid wood floor has shades within it that range from pale to dark, so we chose the darker colors for the paneling to make the room feel that bit more serious. We also restored the client's own desk, which has a top of gaufrage leather. At the desk is a comfortable leather swivel chair—a strong, serious piece of furniture. We gave the side chairs cushions in green and gold to pick up the colors of the walls and the gilding on the desk and to echo the green and gold of the adjacent living room (see pages 78–83).

TOP LEFT, ABOVE LEFT, AND ABOVE: *The side chairs have cushions in a green and gold weave piped and buttoned in gold.*

LEFT: *A room for serious contemplation with few distracting elements. Everything blends in discreetly, from the leather-topped desk to the gilded picture frame for the icon.*

retreats

I think bedrooms should be luxurious, calming spaces that

reflect the personalities of their owners, and neither too frilly

and feminine, nor black leather macho. Beds should be as

big as possible and supremely comfortable, with the best

linen you can afford, and there should always be more

storage than you think you will need.

ABOVE: *A mirror-clad bedside table takes up no space at all visually but provides a great deal of useful storage.*

LEFT: *With cream walls, a white rug, and light-colored curtains, plus accents in soft gray-blue, this bedroom is a good example of a calming palette.*

Calm, crisp, and elegant

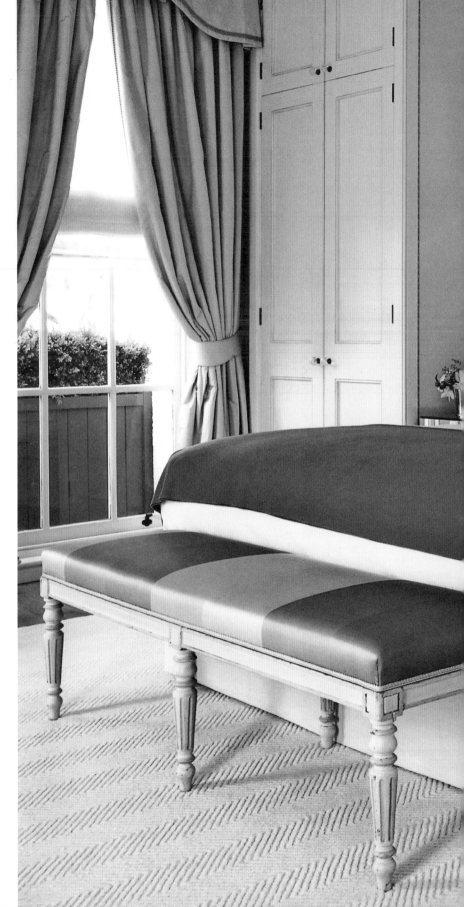

RIGHT: *This upholstered headboard blends into the fabric-covered walls and makes the whole room seem bigger. As well as the elegant and discreet lamps on the bedside tables, there are adjustable swing-arm reading lights on the wall.*

ABOVE: *The neat, flat valances in the bedroom shown on the previous pages are edged with a simple braid to emphasize the lovely curve.*

RIGHT: *The cream fabric on the walls of the same bedroom is a linen from my collection called* Twist. *I have defined the walls and ceiling with a rope that picks up the subtle colors of the room.*

Even simple trimmings add definition

ABOVE: *My* Manchu
*wallpaper is not a
children's pattern, but has
a delightful design of boys
with balloons. Children tire
very quickly of footballers,
ballerinas, wizards, and
fairies. A soft lilac-blue is a
good color for either sex.*

charming but not childish

Children's rooms have to be safe and comfortable, but they also need to grow with the child. When babies are very young and their wardrobes consist of only a handful of babygrows, it is easy to forget about all the storage that will be needed later on.

A young child's room needs to be quiet and also soft on the knees, so a carpet is a good idea. A window treatment that blocks out the light is also advisable.

When considering the color scheme, try to avoid the temptation to go all babyish, as children grow so quickly out of the nursery stage. A neutral, pretty scheme is the ideal to aim for. For the same reason, choose flexible furniture that can be adapted over the years. You can then accessorize the room with lampshades, bedcovers, pictures, and rugs that can easily and inexpensively be changed as the child grows older. If there is space, a spare bed or sofa bed is a useful addition, as it is a good place to curl up for a bedtime story and will soon also come in handy for sleepovers.

LEFT AND BELOW LEFT:
*The braid trim and
checked lining of the
cream wool curtains, as
well as the rope tie-backs,
pick up colors from the
plaid walls.*

RIGHT: *The headboard is
upholstered in the same
cream wool as used for
the bed skirt and also the
curtains. It is piled with
crisp linen pillows—and
one plaid pillow.*

PREVIOUS PAGES: *The plaid
bedroom reflected in the
wall of mirrored closets.*

a stylish plaid hideaway

Plaid, like paisley and chintz, is a great decorating classic, but you need to
treat it as you would any powerful pattern—with caution. A bold plaid fabric
battened onto the walls is the main act in this bedroom, and everything else
is quite plain. The cream-colored curtains have a red and green braid trim
on the leading edges, to pick up on the colors of the plaid. We lined the
curtains with a check, so that the stripes and squares are a constant theme
but are not overdone.

LEFT AND ABOVE: *You do not have to stick to dark, masculine woods when decorating with plaid—this pretty chair and delicate campaign stool look just as good. I particularly like the romantic mix of the Scottish plaid with the Italian furniture belonging to the owner.*

a room full of personality

In this bedroom plaid makes a superb background to the collection of gilt-framed pictures and prints. These, in turn, help to break up the expanse of plaid, as do the large windows and wall of mirrored closet doors. The red accent is picked up in the upholstery of the comfortable armchair and the side chair as well as the red flowers by the bed and in the tall, elegant vase on the desk.

This room is a very strong plaid statement, but the walls do not overwhelm because of all the neutrals that keep the plaid in check. It is a cozy and stylish masculine hideaway with a luxurious feel.

making the most of an awkward shape

Sliced from a larger room, this bedroom ended up being long, thin, and rather tall. In conversions—or even in new houses—awkward shapes and sizes of rooms are often a headache. My solution to disguising difficult proportions is to use an all-over wallpaper and fabric pattern.

This guest bedroom was also awkward to furnish because the only place for the bed was with its side against a wall, which is why we went for the French daybed look. We found a bed with head and foot boards of equal height so it would look like the arms of a sofa. In order to make it look a little narrower, we put bolsters down the back and sides, along with plenty of pillows.

The lighting—reading lamps on adjustable arms—will work equally well whether the bed is used as a sofa or as a bed.

ABOVE LEFT AND ABOVE: *Soft whites and grays work well with pale blue. Bolsters and pillows give the bed a real sofa feel.*

RIGHT: *My* Bovary *fabric and wallpaper used on the bed and walls disguises the awkward proportions of this room. The cane-ended daybed solves the problem of where to put the bed.*

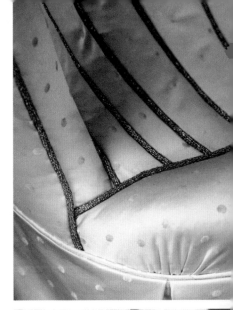

LEFT: *A thick silk rope holds back the cream silk curtains. The tie-back picks up the blue background of my* Bovary *wallpaper and fabric.*

RIGHT: *A glass-bead piping cord defines the scallop-shell design of this pretty side chair.*

BELOW RIGHT: *A harmonious trim: three colors of bobble on the lampshade reflect the tones of the room.*

BOTTOM RIGHT: *On the hem of the side chair, a pearl and silver-bead trim picks up on the glass-bead piping and the white self-patterned fabric.*

Have fun with finishing touches

braiding, beading, and bobbles

Every bedroom needs an element of fun and a dash of individuality. I am a big fan of beads, braids, and bobbles, which are great ways to finish off fabrics, tie back curtains, and add detail to any room. You can choose a trim that exactly matches your fabric (an effect that can either be very boring or very smart); one that harmonizes with your color palette; or one that completely contrasts.

Harmonies are good for creating calm and restful rooms such as bedrooms, and that is the approach we took in this bedroom, in which all the trimmings are from my collection. A wealth of trims are available today. Alternatively, because many trimmings are handmade, you can often take in samples of your fabrics and have trims made up to bring everything together.

Contrasts are dramatic and need to be handled with care and flair. They can be used to define the lines of furniture, highlight smart tailoring, or emphasize horizontal or vertical lines within the room. For example, you could use a rope trim on a wall to make the eye travel upward and raise the apparent height of the ceiling, or you could define the horizontals to concentrate the eye on the width of the room.

the recycled bedroom

Of course, this room is not actually recycled, but it is designed around what was already there when my client bought the apartment. The walls were covered with a chocolate-brown grass paper, and there was a cream carpet. The client wanted a blue and white bedroom, and because blues, whites, and chocolate browns are a great combination, we decided to build the scheme around them.

The first task was to find a fabric with all three colors in it, and I discovered a lovely old Bernard Neville chintz to anchor the scheme. Apart from the glorious and striking Parsua rug that we bought to cover the cream carpet, almost everything else is blue or white, which keeps the scheme interesting.

I am a firm believer in working out what you already have that you can incorporate, and I think this philosophy is coming through more strongly every year. Of course, you want to live in a house that reflects your own taste and personality, but there are so many ways of taking even something as distinctive as chocolate-brown grass paper and making it your own. And including "vintage" elements gives a room layers and a sense of history.

LEFT: *A soft blue fabric covered in lace picks up on the blue in the chintz curtains and revitalizes an antique dressing table. Traditional dressing tables like this are enjoying a revival, and can be very beautiful. If you are lucky enough to have an old one, you could transform it by giving it a new skirt.*

RIGHT: *The carved and gilded headboard was attached to a regular bed, marrying comfort and style, while the bedside cupboard was custom-made and painted.*

fabrics and furniture

The decoration for a bedroom is focused around three large, dominating items—the bed, cupboards (or other storage space), and curtains. In most bedrooms there is relatively little space left for other furniture.

Yet the bedroom is also more than a place to sleep. It serves as a sanctuary, as your ultimate private space. It is your backstage dressing room where you prepare for the drama of life, so it needs plenty of storage and good lighting. Remember, too, that bedroom decoration is not just a nighttime issue—you will be using the room during the day as well, so if you can, let the sun shine in. Good daylight is one of the loveliest things you can have in the bedroom.

LEFT: *A closer look at the lace and silk skirt around the antique dressing table. Lace was rather swept away on the tide of minimalism, but, like so many decorative elements, it is coming back. Anything that spells quality and craftsmanship will always stand the test of time —if you do not want something to look dated, buy the best.*

BELOW LEFT: *On the dressing table, the gathered lace beneath the glass top provides an unusual textural effect. I loved restoring this piece to play its part again. A similar effect could be created on any dressing table.*

RIGHT: *Sometimes it is just great fun to go over the top, as in this wonderful pair of tassel tie-backs, made especially to pick up all the colors of the fabric.*

Decorate your bedroom for both day and night

RIGHT: *This pretty room has comfort at its heart. The use of the same fabric on the headboard and bed skirt as on the walls creates a spacious feel, making the bed less dominant.*

Pull the elements together with a single pattern

romantic bedrooms

The balance between comfort and style is at its most crucial in bedrooms. Because a large, comfortable bed, cosseting bedlinen, good lighting, and plenty of storage are all essential, this usually leaves relatively little space for anything else. Bedrooms are probably the most crowded rooms in the house, and you need to remember this when decorating.

Keeping it simple, however, does not have to mean forgoing pattern and color—here I have used one pattern and a theme of rose and cream to pull everything together. The pattern is romantic and delicate, but not too busy, and I have used it on the walls, headboard, bed skirt, curtains, and chair, while keeping everything else—lampshades, bedlinen, even the bedside tables—plain. The effect is to pull several diverse elements together. Similarly, the scalloped edges of the bedside tables and bedcover echo the curved shape of the headboard, but I have kept other decorative detail to a minimum.

LEFT AND ABOVE: *Small-scale prints can be used on almost anything, from bed skirts, headboards, and valances to chair backs and pillows. However, they look most fresh and modern when partnered with fairly calm accessories, such as cream lampshades, and accented in their deepest color, as in the deep pink here. For finishing touches on smaller-scale patterns, go for simplicity. Here, plain rope is used to define the edges of the walls as well as the shape of the headboard.*

making romantic patterns work

Smaller-scale designs, such as spriggy flowers, work differently from larger ones because they can be used more widely. If you have a valance or a chair back in a big swirling pattern, it may be difficult not to cut the pattern off in its prime or slice a major motif in half. Smaller patterns avoid this problem and so can be used everywhere. This applies to many of the classic romantic designs, such as toiles de Jouy as well as the smaller flower prints. You have a choice—either cover everything in the room or just use the design on a few selected elements such as the walls, in which case be careful how you introduce other patterns. Romantics are best partnered with solid colors, stripes, or checks.

ABOVE: *Silver photo frames, a pretty inlaid box, and a crystal vase of pale pink roses are perfect accessories for the romantic bedroom.*

LEFT: *The strength of color of this tablecloth adds a defining point to the room.*

RIGHT: *This shows that a small print can be used in quite a large room—the screen is marking the division between the dressing room and the bedroom.*

LEFT: *This bed leaves only a tiny space on either side but is supremely inviting. Guests need a full set of pillows and good bedlinen. The walls are papered with my* Manchu *wallpaper, and the curtains are in my* Dromana *linen.*

RIGHT: *This small shower room is classically styled but ergonomically cutting-edge.*

the guest bedroom

Guest rooms and spare rooms can turn into sad and neglected storerooms, or be used as depositories for bits and pieces no one wants anywhere else in the house. A lovely guest room, however, is the first step in making a guest feel welcome. Equally, a room that is prettily decorated but uncomfortable to sleep in will mean your guests go home feeling as if they have done a transatlantic overnight flight. Guests need a comfortable, generous bed (this one almost fills the room but still looks good), plenty of pillows, high-quality bedlinens, and an extra blanket. Curtains should look good but should also keep out the light when closed, and if there is a small shower room, or even just a sink, your guests will relax completely.

ABOVE AND RIGHT: *Unashamed luxury with shiny surfaces, silks, satins, and crystal drops. The chaise in the foreground is the* Mae *chaise from my furniture collection.*

a contemporary classic

This large bedroom is in a light-filled New York apartment with floor-to-ceiling windows along one side. To make the bed into an intimate space within the room, I found a mirrored art deco-style four-poster bed and added a ruched canopy and curtain in a pale self-patterned voile called *Mystery Moon*, from my collection The walls are covered in a striped fabric to add coziness to the room. The curtain fabric is a glamorous printed silk, *Pemberley*, also from my collection.

small space, big impact

This is the powder room that is off the hallway of the Greek house shown on pages 42–5. The woodwork of the hallway and adjacent lobby is painted in a dark green lacquer and I wanted to make sure that, when glimpsed from the cool, dark room beyond, this little sliver of space would have an impact that added to the calm, oriental feel of the hallway. I did not want it to be a tangle of brutal modern plumbing, but to feel like an anteroom.

The white sink is set into a mirrored cabinet that was made to fit the space, and the pale tiles on the floor and walls reflect the light. Above the tiled surround, I used one of my wallpapers, *Macao*, because there is a hint of green in it that echoes the green lacquer in the hallway and lobby. The top of the mirrored cabinet has to be kept uncluttered or the whole Zen feeling of the space would be lost under a sea of hand lotion and colored soaps. Glass vanity tops are not the most practical of surfaces as they show water marks, but they cannot be bettered for visual impact.

ABOVE AND ABOVE RIGHT: *Details of the contemporary Venetian mirror above the sink and the rail of crisp hand towels awaiting use.*

LEFT: *I like the way you can see the black and white marble flooring of the hallway reflected in the cabinet. There are no handles on the cabinet doors; they open with a touch magnetic catch—so much neater.*

*Cool,
calm,
and
spacious*

RIGHT: *The cool, clear spaces of the master bathroom of a house in Greece.*

ABOVE: *Mirroring creates a trompe l'oeil shaped top on these satinwood cupboards, echoing the shape of the over-scaled mirrors above the pair of sinks. It makes a splendid backdrop for a glass and gilt Bagues chandelier—the height of bathroom luxury.*

a master bathroom

A big bathroom is a real luxury. This one has space enough to spare, with a freestanding, double-ended rolltop tub and two generous vanity sinks facing each other. Because of all the drawers in the vanity cabinets (storage again) there is no need to clutter up surfaces, so the room is a calm and relaxing place to be. Over-scaled mirrors above the sinks emphasize the generous proportions. In a large bathroom you can use oversized tiles, like these large Thassos marble slabs, which with their strong lines make the room look even more spacious. The Greek key pattern around the edge of the floor is in Ming marble, as is the vanity top.

distributors

Nina Campbell's fabric and wallpaper collections are distributed throughout the world by OSBORNE & LITTLE

Visit: www.osborneandlittle.com for stockists and details of agents' showrooms.
Email oandl@osborneandlittle.com.

UK
UK Head Office
(For general enquiries)
OSBORNE & LITTLE
Riverside House
26 Osiers Road
London SW18 1NH
Tel: +44 (0)20 8812 3000

UK Showroom
(Open to the trade and public)
OSBORNE & LITTLE
304 King's Road
London SW3 5UH
Tel: +44 (0)20 7352 1456

USA
USA Head Office
(For general enquiries)
OSBORNE & LITTLE INC.
90 Commerce Road
Stamford, CT 06902
Tel: +1 (0)203 3591500

FRANCE
(Trade showroom by appointment only)
OSBORNE & LITTLE
7 rue de Furstemberg
75006 Paris
Tel: +33 (0)1 56 81 02 66

(General enquiries)
Tel: +33 (0)1 55 69 81 06

GERMANY
(General enquiries)
Tel: +49 (0)69 50 98 51 71

NINA CAMPBELL FURNITURE
Distributed by
ARTHUR BRETT & SONS LTD

UK & Europe Head Office
Tel: +44 (0)20 7730 7304
Fax: + 44 (0)20 7730 7105
USA Head Office
Tel: + 1 (0)336 886 7102
Fax: +1 (0)336 886 7078

LAMBSWOOL THROWS
Distributed by JOHNSTONS

UK & Europe Head Office
Tel: +44 (0)1343 554000
USA Distributor
Tel: 800 544 5966
Fax: 336 887 3334

WALL TO WALL CARPETS
Distributed by WOOL CLASSICS

UK & Europe Head Office
Tel: +44 (0)20 7349 1560
Distributed by SAXONY
USA Distributor
Tel: +1 (0)212 755 7100

NINA CAMPBELL HOME FRAGRANCE
Distributed by HOME 360

UK & Europe Office
Tel: +44 (0)20 7491 8877
Fax: +44 (0)20 7491 8878
USA Head Office
Tel: +1 (0)713 344 1665
Fax: +1 (0)713 344 1784

NINA CAMPBELL LINENS
Wholesale contact FIONA MCKELVIE
Tel: +44 (0)20 8488 5984
Fax: +44 (0)20 8488 5984

Nina's address book

ANTIQUES

B + T ANTIQUES
118 Talbot Road
London W11 1JR
England
+44 (0)20 7229 7001
www.bntantiques.co.uk

BIRGIT ISRAEL
251—253 Fulham Road
London SW3 6HY
England
+44 (0)20 7376 7255
www.birgitisrael.com

CARLTON DAVIDSON
507 Kings Road
London SW10 0TX
England
+44 (0)20 7795 0905
www.carltondavidson.co.uk

GUINEVERE ANTIQUES
574–580 Kings Road
London SW6 2DY
England
+44 (0)20 7736 2917
www.guinevere.co.uk

BATHROOMS

BATHROOMS INTERNATIONAL
4 Pont Street
London SW1X 9EL
England
+44 (0)20 7838 7788
www.bathroomsint.com

CARPETS AND RUGS

PARSUA
70 South Audley Street
London W1K 2RA
England
+44 (0)20 7493 5288
www.cb-parsua.com

STARK CARPET
3rd Floor, South Dome
Chelsea Harbour Design
Centre
Chelsea Harbour
London SW10 0XE
England
+44 (0)20 7352 6001
www.starkcarpet.com

CONSTRUCTION

CHERRYWOOD CONTRACTS
2 Station Parade
Cherry Tree Rise
Buckhurst Hill
Essex IG9 6EU
England
+44 (0)20 8505 0150

RUDGARD CITY
8 Fairfax Place
London W14 8HN
England
+44 (0)20 7602 1610

CURTAIN FITTINGS

MCKINNEY AND CO
Studio P
The Old Imperial Laundry
71 Warriner Gardens
London SW11 4XW
England
+44 (0)20 7627 5077
www.mckinney.co.uk

FABRICS

CLAREMONT
35 Elystan Street
London SW3 3NT
England
+44 (0)20 7581 9575
www.claremontfurnishing.com

LELIÈVRE
108–110 Chelsea Harbour
Design Centre
Chelsea Harbour
London SW10 0XE
England
+44 (0)20 7352 4798
www.lelievre.eu

NYA NORDISKA
132—134 Lots Road
London SW10 0RJ
England
+44 (0)800 069 9610
www.nya.com/en

PIERRE FREY
107 Design Center East
1st Floor Chelsea Harbour
London SW10 0XF
England
+44 (0)20 7376 5599
www.pierrefrey.com

SAHCO HESSLEIN
G24 Chelsea Harbour
Design Centre
Chelsea Harbour
London SW10 0XE
England
+44 (0)20 7352 6168
www.sahco.com

TISSUS D'HÉLÈNE
421 The Chambers
Chelsea Harbour
London SW10 0XF
England
+44 (0) 20 7352 9977
www.tissusdhelene.co.uk

TURNELL & GIGON
410 The Chambers
Chelsea Harbour Design
  Centre
Chelsea Harbour
London SW10 OXE
England
+44 (0)20 7259 7280
www.tandggroup.com

ZIMMER & ROHDE
15 Chelsea Harbour
  Design Centre
Chelsea Harbour
London SW10 OXE
England
+44 (0)20 7351 7115
www.zimmer-rohde.com

FLOORING

(See also Carpets and Rugs)

AA FLOORING
24 Howard Close Business
Park
Waltham Abbey
Essex EN9 1XE
England
+44 (0)1992 769100

ELEMENT 7
Unit 2
Parsons Green Depot
Parsons Green Lane
London SW6 4HH
England
+44 (0)20 7736 2366
www.element7.co.uk

FLOWERS

JOHN CARTER FLOWERS
Unit 12a The 1927 Building
2 Michael Road
London SW6 2AD
England
+44 (0)20 7731 5146
www.johncarterflowers.com

FURNITURE AND
FURNITURE MAKING

(See also Garden Furniture)

BEN WHISTLER
9 Silver Road
London W12 7SG
England
+44 (0)20 8576 6600
www.benwhistler.com

CHRISTOPHER CLARK
Sovereign Way
Trafalgar Industrial Estate
Downham Market
Norfolk PE38 9SW
England
+44 (0)1366 389400
www.christopherclark.co.uk

JULIA GRAY
D&D Building
979 3rd Avenue
New York, NY 10022
USA
+1 (0)212 223 4454
www.juliagrayltd.com

MANBORNE
Unit 5, Valley Farm
Reeds Lane
Sayers Common
Hassocks
West Sussex BN6 9JQ
England
+44 (0)1273 831131

NIERMANN WEEKS
60 Generals Highway
Millersville
MD 21108
USA
+1 (0)410 923 0123
www.niermannweeks.com

PARSON'S TABLE
362 Fulham Road
London SW10 9UU
England
+44 (0)20 7352 7444
www.theparsonstablecompany
.com

TAILLARDAT
955 rue des Bruyères
45075 Orléans
France
+33 (0)2 38 51 24 03
www.taillardat.fr

WILLIAM YEOWARD
270 Kings Road
London SW3 5AW
England
+44 (0)20 7349 7828
www.williamyeoward.com

GALLERIES AND
STUDIOS

(See also Glass Decoration)

DNA DESIGN
Core 1, The Gasworks
2 Michael Road
London SW6 2ER
England
+44 (0)20 7751 0022

LUCY B CAMPBELL
GALLERY
123 Kensington Church
Street
London W8 7LP
England
+44 (0)20 7727 2205
www.lucybcampbell.com

PETER ADLER
Pebble
191 Sussex Gardens
London W2 2RH
England
+44 (0)20 7262 1775
www.pebblelondon.com

GARDEN DESIGN
STEPHEN WOODHAMS
45 Elizabeth Street
London SW1W 9PA
+44 (0)20 7730 3353
www.woodhams.co.uk

GARDEN FURNITURE
MCKINNON AND HARRIS
1806 Summit Avenue
Richmond
Virginia 23220-1109   USA
+1 (0)804 358 2385
www.mckinnonandharris.com

GLASS DECORATION
GUILLAUME SAALBURG
Techniques
Transparentes
99 rue Molière
94200 Ivry-sur-Seine
France
+33 (0)1 71 33 05 05
www.techniquestransparentes
.com

KITCHENS
KITCHEN CENTRAL
19 Carnwath Road
London SW6 3EN
England
+44 (0)20 7736 6458

LIGHTING
DAVID BUTLER
31 Richmond Way
London W14 OAS
England
+44 (0)20 7603 2254

FORBES AND LOMAX
205a St Johns Hill
London SW11 1TH
England
+44 (0)20 7738 0202
www.forbesandlomax.com

LUCY COPE
Foxhill House
Allington
Chippenham
Wiltshire SN14 6LL
England
+44 (0)1249 650446
www.lucycope.com

LINEN
**MONOGRAMMED LINEN
SHOP**
168 Walton Street
London SW3 3JL
England
+44 (0)20 7589 4033
www.monogrammedlinenshop.com

PAINTING, SPECIALIST PAINTING, DECORATING
CATHERINE CUMMINGS
49 Sydney Street
London SW3 6PX
England
+44 (0)20 7306 2670

HALLMARK DECOR
32 Thames Road
Canvey Island
Essex SS8 0HH
England
+44 (0)1268 696913

JOHN SUMPTER
82 Overstone Road
London W6 OAB
England
+44 (0)20 8748 0992

PICTURE FRAMING AND RESTORATION
CAMPBELL'S OF LONDON
33 Thurloe Place
London SW7 2HQ
England
+44 (0) 20 7584 9268
www.campbellsoflondon.co.uk

PICTURE HANGING
PHOENIX FINE ART
15 Mayday Gardens
London SE3 8NJ
England
+44 (0)20 8319 3527

ROCK CRYSTAL LOGS
CREEL AND GOW
131 East 70th Street
New York, NY 10021
USA
+1 (0)212 327 4281
www.creelandgow.com

TELEVISION AND AUDIO
MUSIC GURU
(Alessandra Nerdrum)
+44 (0)20 7624 3445
www.musicguru.co.uk

SOUND CREATION
(Brocus Burrows)
The Old School
Luckings Estate
Magpie Lane
Coleshill, nr Amersham
Buckinghamshire HP7 0LS
England
+44 (0)1494 434400

WINDOW TREATMENTS, UPHOLSTERY, WALLING

(See also Curtain Fittings)

BRAY DESIGN
Unit 7
Hawes Hill Farm
Drift Road, Winkfield
Berkshire SL4 4QQ
England
+44 (0)1344 890998

EDGE INTERIORS
8 Clarendon Terrace
London W9 1BZ
England
+44 (0)20 7289 1189

www.edgeinteriors.co.uk

GARVEY BROTHERS
39 The Baulk
London SW18 5RA
England
+44 (0)20 8871 1739

J & B CONTRACTS
2A Denbigh Place
London SW1V 2HB
England
+44 (0)20 7622 4614

LEN CARTER
37 Shuttleworth Road
London SW11 3DH
England
+44 (0)20 7228 6676

REVAMP INTERIORS
15 East Place
West Norwood
London SE27 9JW
England
+44 (0)20 8670 5151

www.revampinteriors.co.uk

acknowledgments

With special thanks to all my clients who have been so wonderful to work with and my team—Georg Lauth, Anja Fehling, Ciara Donegan, Lucy Black, and Buffy Benson.

A huge thanks also to Brocus Burrows, The Monogrammed Linen Shop, John Sumpter, Phoenix Fine Art, John Carter, Stephen Woodhams, Peter and Philip Garvey, Len Carter, Guinevere Antiques, Melissa Wyndham, Peter Adler, Alexandra Parsons, Alexandra Campbell, and all those at Cico Books.

index